# My Day

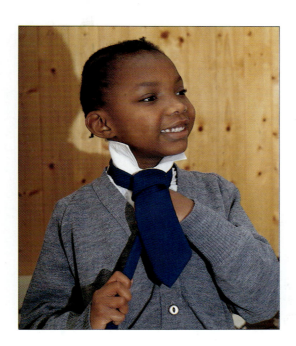

Written by Barrie Wade
Photographed by Paul Moore
Illustrated by Angie Sage

Collins *Educational*
An imprint of HarperCollins *Publishers*

My day starts when I wake up.

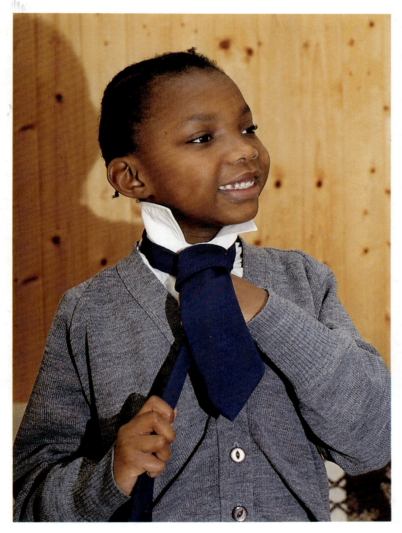

I get dressed for school.

I eat my breakfast,

then I go to school with my sister.

We write in the morning

and we read in the book corner.

Our teacher helps us with maths

and she tells us good stories.

In the afternoon I like to do jigsaws

and make things with paper.

After school Mum
takes us home.

I ride my bike in the garden.

We have dinner.

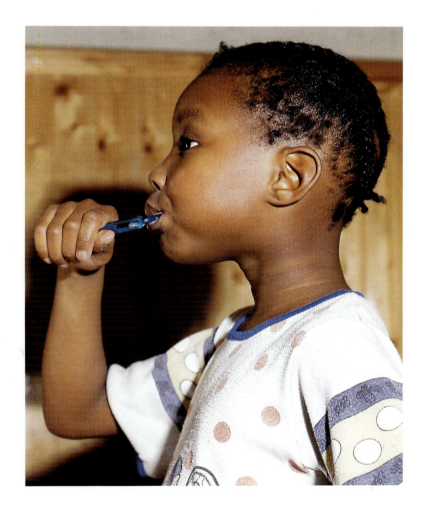

I clean my teeth and then...

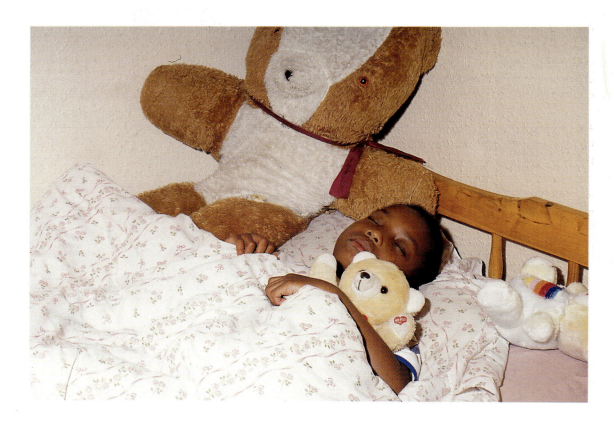

I go to bed.
**That's my day!**